Book Description

"The greatest enemies of success and happiness are negative emotions of all kinds" –
Brian Tracey

Emotions affect every aspect of your life, from how you process information to your interactions with other people. Many don't understand how emotions are formed and accept them as they come, never taking the time to learn how to control and release them. When your body is ruled by negative emotions trapped inside, you attract and perceive experiences resonating with your emotional state.

This book teaches you what emotions are and how they affect your body's physiology and your behaviors. It provides a clear and concise understanding of the science behind emotional responses, from how stimuli travels from the sensory receptors to the brain to how the body responds to stressors. It explains how the brain uses energy and frequency to communicate information within the body before introducing the reader to various sound therapy and breathwork techniques that can help you release trapped negative emotions. Most of these techniques have been used to improve physical and mental health by civilizations dating as far back as antiquity and across the religious and spiritual spectrum. They are all easily accessible, affordable, and backed by scientific study.

If you are looking for an informative, easy-to-understand read that successfully combines New Age spiritualism with science, then this is the book for you.

Release Trapped Negative Emotions with Sound and Breathwork

Raise Your Vibration into a Positive State of Mind and Clear Away Feelings of Stress, Anxiety, Fear and Resentment.

Geoffrey Thomas

Table of Contents

Introduction

"Let's not forget that the little emotions are the great captains of our lives and we obey them without realizing it." –Vincent Van Gogh

We are all beholden to our emotions. They help us navigate everyday life by prompting us to respond to the situations and people we encounter. Emotions play an important role in our survival because they can signal possible danger or help us have a deeper enjoyment of positive experiences. They can be overwhelming and if you allow them to run rampant, they will taint your ability to think rationally. The most prominent emotions in your being affect your perspective on life and how you interact with others.

Every person on earth can think of at least one occasion where they were faced with an unexpected and unpleasant situation eliciting negative emotions from them that had a ripple effect on their lives. Say for example you are unexpectedly forced to relocate to a city you were never fond of. Your instinctive response to this may be anger at the disruption to your schedule or fear at the thought of being alone in an unfamiliar environment. You don't get the chance to process and release these emotions because you are focused on packing up, settling into a new place, and then focusing on your work as a way to distract yourself. Months go by and every encounter you have in the new town seems to be negative because you haven't released those emotions of anger or fear. You're always in a bad mood because of this and the people you meet in the new town seem unfriendly towards you and say you have a 'bad vibe'. The lack of positive social interaction coupled with your continually bad mood makes you depressed. After a few years, nothing has changed for the better and you feel that moving to this town turned you into a depressed person.

All of this is an unfortunate series of events that began with negative emotions you never released. A scenario like this is all too common because most people aren't conscious of their emotions and simply accept them as they come, never thinking to rationalize through them. We forget that we embody the energy within and around us and if you're filled with negative energy, it will attract more negativity and continue this cycle until you make a conscious decision to break it. Negative energy drains us and we can't live our lives to the fullest while carrying it around.

Emotions And Our Stress Response

Your truest, most authentic self embodies bliss, peace, and tranquility. When a threat to this natural state presents itself, negative emotions alert us to it. We are meant to consider these emotions only as an alarm system prompting us to address the threat so we can return to our naturally blissful state. Unfortunately, most of us don't know how to analyze these emotions or determine the kind of action we need to take to combat the threat so we can release them. Instead, we centre our personalities on these emotions, labelling ourselves as angry or cowardly people. The brain's inability to distinguish between real and perceived threats only serves to exacerbate this state of affairs as it responds to both with the same intensity.

Our stress response, also known as the "fight, flight, or freeze" response, was coded into our DNA during the prehistoric times of primitive man. Animal attacks, unprecedented weather, and poisonous plants were the greatest threats to our survival and each one required immediate action. We had to intuitively and hastily decide which reaction gave us the greatest chance of survival, whether it be running from or fighting a charging animal, retching up poisonous plants we had eaten, or hiding from strong winds and violent thunderstorms. These responses are ingrained into our brains before we have the ability to think rationally. They form memories conditioning us to stay away from certain environments. These memories inform how we react to a similar threat in the future.

Society and External Stimuli

Today's society has advanced to the point where we are, for the most part, removed from situations requiring an immediate and visceral reaction to protect our survival. Despite this, our brains still elicit the same response to any perceived threat. These responses often put unnecessary stress on our bodies that can cause illnesses with adverse long term effects. If the perceived threat is not real or doesn't require a strong and overpowering reaction, we are left with the unnecessarily triggered physiological effects of the stress response in our bodies. Our lifestyles only encourage us to address the symptoms of the illnesses caused by these physiological changes. Unfortunately, this is an ineffective healing approach because we don't address the root of the issue. This is why you find yourself treating the same diseases for years on end without any significant improvements. This is not to say you should shun modern medicine, but you can only benefit from implementing both approaches.

The structure of modern society has us constantly exposed to a barrage of external stimuli, most of which are negative. Our lifestyles make it almost impossible for us to take the time to acknowledge our emotions and our brains still have not evolved to a place where they can instinctively distinguish a real threat to our survival from an uncomfortable or stressful circumstance. This leaves us inundated with negative emotions that become trapped in our bodies. They create blockages in our aura, lowering our vibrations because they prevent energy from flowing through and within us. The lowered vibrations manifest in our bodies as bad moods, depression, digestive issues, heart palpitations, anxiety, and so forth. It's often difficult for us to figure out what the root cause of these maladies is. After spending a few minutes unsuccessfully trying to filter through the emotional debris, we often resign ourselves to these conditions and continue with our lives as usual.

We must learn how to understand and recognize our emotions so we can release the negative energy they carry. This doesn't mean we rush to erase these emotions so we can focus only on the positive ones. Instead, we need to sit with the feelings and evaluate them. We need to understand what triggered them so we can address the problem(s) and put the emotion to rest by releasing it from our bodies. Once we've mastered this, we will have a lighter mental state, a deeper connection to our higher self, and improved physical health.

Raising Your Vibrations: What You Will Learn

Raising our awareness and being conscious of every aspect of our being is the key to an improved quality of life. We need to understand how our minds, bodies, and spirits are connected in an intricate network of nerves, sensory receptors, and electromagnetic fields. This knowledge gives us the tools we need to successfully raise our vibrations and release the unwanted negative emotions blocking positive energy from freely flowing in and through our bodies.

This book aims to teach you how to overcome negative emotions through inexpensive alternative healing methods backed by science. Emotions are energy and the methods included in this book focus on manipulating the frequency of your brain's energy and mindfully controlling your breathing patterns to facilitate the release of negative emotions. You will learn what emotions are and how they influence both your physiology and behavioral patterns. You will also learn how the brain's structure contributes to your emotional responses and the effect of emotions on your physical and spiritual bodies. The book then moves to explain frequency, the body's electromagnetic field, and the electrical signals communicating information through the body. This section ends with a guide on raising your vibrations and how the mind-body connection facilitates this. Finally, it provides various inexpensive and easily accessible sound therapy and breathwork techniques you can use to release trapped negative emotions and raise your vibrations.

Chapter 1: What Are Emotions?

If you want to lead a healthy and well-balanced life, then you need to know how to navigate a variety of situations with some degree of emotional intelligence. This requires you to understand the purpose of emotions and how they present themselves in your body so you can effectively control them. Emotions are our body's response to the external stimuli we encounter in our daily lives and each one elicits a unique physiological reaction prompting us to behave in a specific way. These behaviors communicate our emotions to others and determine how we interact and respond to the people and situations around us.

Stimuli, Reaction, And Behavior

We know that every interaction we have with people and our environment stimulates some kind of reaction from us. This reaction can be joyful, sad, angry or ambivalent. Stimuli relaxing the body or affirming our needs trigger positive emotions like happiness, excitement, and gratitude. Conversely, stimuli that cause distress to the body and trigger our primal survival instincts elicit negative emotions such as anger, fear, and anxiety and are referred to as stressors. Deadlines, financial insecurity, traumatic experiences, unexpected life changes, death, conflict, and physical danger are some of the most common stressors we experience.

The information we receive from external stimuli is communicated to us through our sensory receptors. It's then translated into our brains through neurotransmitters. Each part of the brain will signal the secretion of different hormones and chemicals depending on how it thinks you need to react to the stimuli in question. This is why you can feel the blood rushing to your extremities when you are angry, are sweating and hyperventilating when you are nervous, or have a sense of calm wash over you when you feel relieved. People's physiological responses to the same stimuli can be vastly different based on how their brains process them. For example, an unexpected delay in a project may cause a slight irritation for one person while sending another into a full-blown anxiety attack.

The physiological response will also trigger a physical expression in the form of behavior. Behaviors are how the body communicates our feelings to other people. This can be a smile to express joy, a scream to express anger, or running away to express fear. Behaviors caused by emotions manifest differently from person to person in part because they are meant as a communication tool between us and other people. They are influenced by a myriad of factors, such as personal views and beliefs, preconceived biases and cultural norms, and social conditioning because the person at the receiving end of the behavior needs to understand what you are trying to communicate. For example, when you slurp your food in Japan, people understand this as a sign of enjoyment and a compliment to the chef. This behavior is seen as uncouth in the West so your intention won't be efficiently communicated.

The journey from our body's reception of external stimuli to the physical manifestation of behavioral patterns is a long and complicated chain reaction with a lot of moving parts and yet the whole process happens in a matter of seconds.

Basic and Complex Emotions

We experience two kinds of emotions: basic or complex. Complex emotions are an amalgamation of various feelings that can be boiled down to one or more basic emotions. Emotional psychology theorists generally accept the six basic emotions identified by Paul Ekman. These are anger, sadness, disgust, fear, surprise, and happiness. Their determining factor is they are universally recognized by the same facial expressions, regardless of culture or geography. For example, a smile represents joy or happiness and a scowl represents sadness or displeasure. If you see someone with these facial expressions, you will understand what they are feeling even if you cannot verbally communicate with them. Ekman's research on the universality of emotions was widely accepted until 2014 when a study by the University of Glasgow suggested there are only four basic emotions as some of them behaviorally present themselves in similar ways (Jack *et al*, 2014). The study analyzed the facial muscles used to signal emotions to others and found both fear and surprise are signalled by wide-open eyes in the early signaling stage. Likewise, it found that anger and disgust are both signalled by a wrinkled nose. These behaviors are meant to increase our chances of survival by minimizing the inhalation of harmful particles, signalling a challenge to fight or increasing our visual intake of information from the environment.

Basic emotions are experienced as a reflex to external stimuli. In contrast, complex emotions require logical processing and are expressed by a variety of facial expressions. This is because complex emotions often try to adequately express more than one basic emotion at the same time. For example, grief can be a mix of fear, anger, and sadness while excitement can express happiness and surprise. This makes it difficult to tell which emotion is being expressed purely based on facial expressions, even in expressions made by the same person. For example, you may express grief by crying because you miss a loved one. Tomorrow, you can express that same grief by punching a wall because you're angry your loved one was taken away from you.

Our basic emotions are an instinctual response to stimuli so when our brains encounter complex situations, they can fire off conflicting signals causing us to freeze because we are unsure of how to proceed. This gives us the opportunity to process the nuances of the situation and decide how we feel and how we can communicate this feeling to others. How we choose to express complex emotions is often not universally recognizable because it's based on our past experiences, cultural conditioning, and our determination of what a socially acceptable reaction may be.

The Difference Between Emotions, Feelings, And Moods

People often use the terms emotion, feeling, and mood interchangeably when referring to their reactions to stimuli. However, each term psychologically denotes a different reaction.

Emotions are the raw impulses we feel immediately after receiving stimuli from our sensory receptors. Emotions can be overwhelming and usually prompt an immediate behavioral response that has not been rationalized. The behavior we exhibit in response to an emotional impulse is based on our subjective past experiences. Emotions can also be triggered by our memories. We can all think of instances when we thought of an experience we once had and were immediately overcome by the same emotions we felt during the actual experience. This happens because emotions are signals we receive from the amygdala, which holds our memories. So when you recall a memory, the amygdala responds to it in the same way it would to external stimuli and sends the same impulses to your body.

Feelings are rationalized emotional impulses. They occur when the impulses move from the amygdala into the neocortex which deals with sensory perception, memory, and cognitive thought. The amygdala processes sensory information primarily based on what it perceives to be potential threats of danger. As such, emotional impulses are often a reaction only to the part of the stimuli the amygdala deems a threat. In contrast, the neocortex can process stimuli in a more layered way by evaluating them as a whole and integrating it with logic, memories, and individual experiences. Let's say for example you are about to pitch a new product to a company you've previously worked with. When you arrive at the meeting, you may feel overwhelmed at the number of people also pitching their products and become fearful you will not be successful. These two feelings can be traced back to the basic emotions of fear and sadness. You may be fearful of losing out on a great opportunity to distribute your product and sad you will have to retrench some people working for you because you were relying on the success of this pitch to fund your expenses for the coming quarter. But when you pause to consider the rapport you've built with the company, the quality of your product, and the time you've spent preparing for the pitch, you will start feeling confident. This happens when your neocortex has rationalized the impulses of fear and sadness and replaced them with the feeling of confidence instead.

Moods are a generalized state caused by the watered-down effects of your emotions and feelings. They are not caused by specific stimuli and tend to last much longer than emotions and feelings. Moods can affect how we think and perceive things because of their extended duration. If you are in a bad mood, your disposition towards any stimuli will be equally negative. As a result, you will have negative emotions and feelings towards any new external stimuli and this will prolong your bad mood. The same is true for good moods and positive emotions.

The main differences between emotions, feelings, and moods lie in the sliding scale of the duration and intensity of each. Emotions are much more intense than feelings and tend to last only for a few seconds or minutes. Feelings are not as consuming as emotions and can last anywhere between a few seconds to a few hours. Moods are very dull and most people don't know what kind of mood they are in until they evaluate their day. Because of their passivity, moods can last for hours or even months at a time.

The Brain And Its Role In Emotional Responses

Our brain is the hub translating external triggers into emotional responses so we must have a basic understanding of how it functions in order to have a better grasp on the shift from impulse to behavior. The best way to explain how the brain's structure relates to our emotions and feelings is through the theory of the three brains. This model was developed by neuroscientist Paul MacLean and groups the brain into three layers according to their function.

The first layer is known as the reptilian brain and it consists of the cerebellum and the brain stem. This part of the brain controls basic functions such as breathing, moving, and reproducing. It's programmed to execute impulsive behaviors necessary for survival and triggers the "fight, flight, or freeze" stress response. The reptilian brain's behaviors are genetically programmed and difficult to change. This is the brain layer dominant in situations where we are not actively aware of our thoughts and surroundings.

Next we have the mammalian brain/limbic system. This layer continues from the brain stem and includes the cerebrum, amygdala, hypothalamus, and hippocampus. The limbic system associates emotions with experiences and behaviors which then creates memories. It also controls hormone secretion, blood flow, and body temperature. Its creation and storage of memories allows us to learn and adapt to new environments. The limbic system's connection to the reptilian brain responds to stimuli that triggers survival instincts and forms memories of the situations so it can condition us on how to interact with similar environments in the future.

Lastly, there is the neocortex which encases the previous two sets. This is the part of the brain rationalizing the information we get from our sensory receptors. It applies logic, memory, and past experiences to this information and produces a multi-layered understanding of the situation at hand. The neocortex allows us to plan, speak, and make voluntary movements. When we are actively engaging with our environment, the neocortex usurps dominance from the reptilian brain and allows us to make thought-out decisions.

All of these layers are connected by a network of nerves sending electrical signals from the sensory receptors into the brain. While each layer has its own purpose, they all function collaboratively to create a physically and spiritually sound experience. For example, the limbic system responds to triggers of anger and fear which in turn triggers the "fight, flight, or freeze" response controlled by the reptilian brain. Likewise, the neocortex relies on memories formed by the limbic system for its cognitive functions.

The Emotional Mind And The Thinking Mind

To better understand our emotions and feelings, we can categorize the mind into two: the emotional mind and the thinking mind.

The emotional mind is made up of the reptilian brain and the limbic system. It controls emotions and how our bodies respond to them. This is the part of our brain that conditions us to repeat pleasurable experiences and avoid harmful/painful ones. The emotional mind functions by compartmentalization and cannot perform an intersectional analysis of the situation like the neocortex can. When it recognizes a situation that caused you anxiety in the past, it will automatically respond by making you feel anxious even if that emotion is unnecessary in the present moment. All the 'negative' experiences you've had in the past, your personal beliefs, and social conditioning play a role in how you instinctually respond to stressors. The amygdala connects the limbic system and the brain stem (part of the reptilian brain) and is always on the lookout for potential threats to your survival. When stress signals are sent by the amygdala, they reach the reptilian brain before the neocortex, resulting in immediate and instinctive reactions.

The neocortex makes up the thinking mind because it is the part of the brain using cognitive functions to think, reason, plan, and execute actions. The thinking mind can evaluate complex emotions and come up with strategies and new, more appropriate emotions to situations.

The amygdala is almost fully developed at birth while the neocortex is only 75% developed six months after birth. This means the experiences we have in our childhood are deeply ingrained into our brains because they create pathways in the brain making it difficult to change behaviors and habits we developed during childhood.

The Effect Of Negative Emotions On The Body

When the body is exposed to stressors that elicit emotions of fear and anger, the brain responds by triggering the "fight, flight, or freeze" stress response. This response alerts our body to a perceived threat to our survival and causes hormonal and chemical changes in our bodies preparing us to protect ourselves. The stress response is designed to make you adapt to your environment in the safest way possible. In some cases, the only way to ensure your survival is to fight off the threat. You could also run away from the threat or freeze so you can gather more information from your surroundings before taking action or hiding yourself. This response was coded into the human DNA in primitive times where some of the greatest threats to our survival were animal attacks. Such threats required us to literally run, fight, or hide from them. The threats we face in modern society have more to do with other humans than with wild animals, so your fight response might look like confronting a difficult colleague instead of wrestling with a tiger.

Negative emotions like stress, resentment, and anxiety are all linked to fear and anger so they can also trigger the stress response. For example, anxiety is one of the long term effects of an overactive stress response and stress itself is a direct response to fear.

"Fight, flight, or freeze" is triggered by the signals sent by the amygdala to the hypothalamus. The hypothalamus then activates the autonomic nervous system (ANS) which releases the stress hormones adrenaline and cortisol. These hormones prompt you to go into immediate action, increase glucose production to send to the bloodstream so you have more energy, and limit bodily functions like reproduction or digestion which can take energy away from the muscles, thus slowing your physical movement.

When the stress hormones secrete, the body undergoes some of the following physiological changes:

- Your pupils dilate and your peripheral vision increases so you're able to see your surroundings better.

- Your lung muscles relax so you're able to take deeper breaths and supply more oxygen to the bloodstream.

- Your blood thickens so it can clot more easily should you get injured.

- Your hands and feet will heat up or cool down depending on whether your body has decided to fight, run, or stand still.

- Your perception of pain decreases so your movement is not slowed down.

While the body responds in physiologically predictable ways during the stress response, the behaviors we exhibit differ for each person. If you have experienced trauma, then your stress response will be overactive because you are more sensitive to danger and your brain perceives danger in circumstances where others may not. Let's say you were in a coffee shop when an earthquake hit, entrapping you under a pile of rubble. If all you could smell while you were waiting to be rescued was coffee, then your brain is likely to trigger the stress response whenever it smells coffee.

An overactive "fight, flight, or freeze" response could have long term effects on your health because of the disturbances it causes to the balanced functioning of the body. These include weight gain due to stress eating, having digestive or heart issues, irregular sleep patterns, and prolonged muscle pain. Failing to acknowledge and release the negative emotions caused by external stimuli also contributes to an overactive stress response because the brain never learns how to respond more appropriately to stimuli that are not as life threatening as it had originally perceived. If you don't rationalize and work through your stress response to a certain situation or environment, you will continue having the same reaction each time you encounter it. This puts unnecessary strain on your body and can cause irreparable long term damage.

The Effect Of Negative Emotions On The Spirit

The spirit body is the intangible energy part of our being, the part connecting us to everything in existence and the universe. Being in touch with our spirit requires us to have a balanced disposition. The spirit is healthiest when it is aligned with the emotional and the physical aspects of our being. The mind and body are connected so if the mind can't get you to acknowledge your emotions, it will physically manifest the distress through illness. The more we try to resist our body's signals, the more misaligned our mind and bodies become, and the more dormant our spirit is. The misalignment often happens when we try to suppress our negative emotions instead of acknowledging and releasing them.

Emotions are also made up of energy and negative emotions carry a dense and heavy frequency blocking positive energy from flowing through the body. When negative emotions are trapped in your body, your vibration is lower and you struggle to have a positive perception of life. It's natural to feel these emotions as they are meant to warn us of a threat and make us take action to restore balance in our surroundings or within ourselves. The trouble comes when we don't release these emotions, particularly when the threat is not real because they become trapped in the body and lower our vibrations, making us manifest things with a low frequency. It's easy for negative emotions to remain clogged in the body, mainly because emotional impulses usually occur in the subconscious mind. Another reason for this is our tendency to avoid pain and discomfort as much as possible. We prefer to suppress these emotions and try to manufacture positive ones over them instead of tackling them head on. This is why you'll often hear of people going shopping or out for drinks to 'feel better' instead of addressing their emotions.

Unfortunately, this only serves to store the negative energy in your energy field or aura, which is the body's electromagnetic field. This causes blockages because the dense energy of these emotions prevents other energy from flowing into and through your body. Our bodies act as an amplifier for our emotions so when the electrical signals that communicate emotion to the brain carry dense energy and remain stuck in the body, they are amplified through our aura which resonates with similar energy in our surroundings. Our aura dictates how we experience environments and people and how they experience us. This is why you can attend an event where people generally say they had a good time, but you didn't because you only resonated with the negative moments.

When we are aware of our negative emotions, we can recondition our minds to respond to stressors healthily. We can choose to evaluate our negative emotions using reason and logic instead of suppressing them. This allows us to restructure how we react to the perceived threat or develop a strategy to resolve the stress inducing stimuli. Usually, when we do this, we realize there is no threat or it is minimal and does not require an intense physiological response.

It is no coincidence that undergoing a spiritual awakening and developing emotional intelligence both require us to draw into ourselves and become mindful of how we interact with ourselves, others, and our environment. Both these journeys change how we think which in turn changes our perception of life. The universal truth that there is a sense of pure bliss at the core of the universe and our eternal, highest selves is expressed in almost all variations of enlightenment philosophy. Our understanding of the order and connectivity of all things in existence deepens in tandem with our spiritual awareness and this allows us to appreciate that no perceived threat is insurmountable.

We are connected to our highest selves when our spirit is awakened because our mind, body, and soul are balanced and energy flows through us and improves our connection to everything in existence. This connection brings with it an innate sense of bliss that is unchanged even in moments of adversity, but it's impossible to access this sense of bliss if there are emotional blockages caused by negative energy in the body. Bliss is a positive emotion which vibrates at a higher, lighter frequency than negative emotions. Releasing negative emotions allows us to increase your level of awareness and consciousness, raises our vibrations and allows you to adopt a higher, more positive perspective on life because we can stop our minds from catastrophizing. Awareness lets us recognize our emotions as an alert system warning us of potential danger, instead of an inextricable part of our identity that runs the show. Knowing which basic emotion we are experiencing makes it easier for us to release them because their energy is more fluid. Complex emotions such as resentment, anxiety, depression, and grief are heavier because they are a blend of multiple emotions. If your emotional intelligence is not high, you won't know how to release your emotions and you may even construct your identity based on them. If you often react to situations with anger, you may label yourself as an angry person instead of evaluating why you react this way. Doing this is dangerous and unhealthy because emotions are volatile and often illogical.

The Law Of Resonance And Daily Stimuli

Albert Einstein famously noted that every object, feeling, and being consists of energy vibrating at a certain frequency. The law of resonance states that you attract the kind of energy you embody. So if you embody positive, light energy then you will attract things vibrating at that frequency and vice versa. The law of resonance is closely linked to the law of attraction which states you manifest what you are based on the frequency you emit. The difference between these laws is the former focuses on the energy the subject emits while the latter speaks to the energy of other objects and beings in relation to the subject.

The energy we emit is determined by our disposition and we resonate with the things aligning with our beliefs. Our beliefs are formed by any emotion we attach energy to and create memories based off of and most people define their identities on these beliefs. Oftentimes we are unaware of the core beliefs we hold because they were developed in our youth and they've become second nature to us. These are usually formed while the neocortex was still developing and we were unable to process experiences and emotions through the lens of reason and logic. Whatever basic and distorted notions we create about ourselves and our environment during this time become the distorted beliefs we base our identities on. This is why we need to understand that emotions do not define us. We can unconsciously resonate with the negative energy of our negative beliefs because we are constantly distracted by the unending stressors of daily life.

Stress researcher Mary Wingo writes almost all the diseases present in our society today are a result of the stressful lifestyles of modern society. The continuous stimuli we receive from competitive workplaces, the news, and the effects of an unequal society mean we are always in "fight, flight, or freeze" mode. Before we can fully rationalize and process our negative emotions, another stimulus triggers our stress response and we shift our focus to that, before having the opportunity to unpack and release the earlier emotions and so the cycle continues. This causes prolonged negative moods which are fed back into the environment around us, resonating with the experiences and stimuli emitting equally dense energy. As such, we are only able to perceive life negatively because that is the only energy we resonate with. This same reason is why people who are vibrating at a positive frequency say that they've adopted a higher perspective of life and always seem to be attracting positivity. I'm certain you can think of someone who is always experiencing 'luck' and seems unfazed when they encounter an uncomfortable experience. They've learned how to release negative energy from their bodies and resonate with life in a higher, positive light.

We could say our beliefs become a self-fulfilling prophecy. When we have negative beliefs and are always waiting for something to go wrong, we resonate with fearful energy and manifest this into our daily lives. One of the most common examples of this can be found in people who suffer from anxiety. If you are scared you might fail a test, you may find yourself procrastinating by sleeping more to avoid this feeling or spending most of your time planning your next move if you fail. This means you have less time to study and leads to your failure. You begin to doubt your capabilities and end up paralyzed by inaction because you assume anything you try to do will lead to failure. Time goes by and you see others around you advancing while you are stuck in the same place and this reinforces your belief that you are a failure. When you finally build up the courage to try something new again or challenge yourself again, you spend most of your time procrastinating once more to prepare for the worst. You fail again and so the cycle continues until you can find a way to intentionally rewire your brain and rid yourself of this belief. The anxiety (as a result of its physiological response to perceived threat) also leaves you with digestive and respiratory problems and high blood pressure which negatively affects your quality of life.

You need to understand how the brain functions in relation to your mind and body and how this goes on to affect your spirit. Once you've done that, you can see how the energy emanating from all three aspects influence each other in a way that can be scientifically proven. This is the first step towards becoming self-aware and spiritually conscious.

Chapter 2: Energy And Emotions

"If you want to find the secrets of the universe, think in terms of energy, frequency, and vibration." —Nikola Tesla

Spiritually awakened people have always had a deep understanding of the effects of energy and vibrational frequencies on both the spiritual and physical bodies. Ancient civilizations knew they could draw energy from nature and release it back into the earth. This shows they understood that energy can not be created or destroyed, it can only be transformed and transferred. They also understood the importance of a balanced vibrational frequency in the body. An example of this can be found in the Taoism belief that in order for *qi* to flow freely in the body, the yin and yang had to be balanced because this neutrality means your aura is not blocked by negative energy and has the capacity to absorb positive energy.

Energy is the force behind all forms of life and it powers everything in existence. Everything we can and cannot perceive with our senses is made up of atoms which are constantly moving back and forth. Energy moves in waves and this movement is described using frequency and vibration. Frequency measures how many waves the energy exhibits at any given time while vibration measures how fast these waves are moving. The higher the frequency of matter is, the higher its vibrations.

Frequencies And Auras

Emotions and feelings also have frequencies that can be measured. Low frequency emotions and feelings carry a dense, negative energy that is difficult to move out of while high frequency ones have a lighter, more positive energy.

The emotions with the lowest frequencies include shame, regret, guilt, grief, hopelessness, and apathy. These emotions range from 20 to 80 Hz and they're the heaviest because they compel you to be immobile. When you experience any of these feelings, you want to disappear or shrink yourself as much as possible so you can wallow in despair by yourself. You don't want to move when you are in this state because movement calls attention to you and when you don't move, the energy in your body doesn't move either.

Next on the scales are the emotions of fear, resentment, anger, hostility and pride. These fall in the range of 100 to 175 Hz. These emotions are higher than the previous group because they prompt you to act and so their energy is not as stagnant as that of the first group. However, these emotions are signalled by the reptilian brain and are usually irrational and impulsive. Whatever behavior they elicit from you is most likely to have a negative effect on your life and how people perceive you.

Courage, neutrality, willingness and acceptance are in the middle of the scale with a range of 200 to 350 Hz. These emotions are neutral which means they create space in your aura for light energy to be absorbed.

Reason, motivation, love, happiness, joy and peace are some of the higher frequency emotions ranging from 400 to 600 Hz. These emotions elicit a sense of contentment from you because you are comfortable and feel affirmed and valued in this range.

Lastly, there is the 600 to 700 Hz range that includes bliss, connection, and exhilaration, with the highest being enlightenment. Enlightenment is a state of mind more than it is an emotion because it is the total awareness of the connectedness of everything in existence and the understanding of divine order and timing. This state surpasses emotion because emotion is meant to help us learn, understand, and assimilate with our environment. When you are enlightened, you realize that life is both meaningful and fleeting and you understand every circumstance you experience serves a greater good in the end. This wisdom allows you to release the need to assimilate. Unlike the other feelings and emotions, enlightenment is permanent and cannot be artificially manufactured.

The lowest frequencies of them all come from the feeling of death and actual death. When a person feels death looming over them, they are actually feeling their life force slowly slipping away. There is no energy left in their physical bodies when they are dead.

What Is An Aura?

I've mentioned your body has an electromagnetic field called an energy field or an aura, but what does this mean exactly? Like all electromagnetic fields, your aura is a conduit that attracts energy. Most people can't see the aura but they can feel it in the same way they feel their own emotions. The body's nervous system communicates information through electrical signals and this is how emotions are communicated to the body. Research has also proven all the cells in our bodies produce electromagnetic waves when they vibrate. This confirms the spiritualists' belief that we're able to feel the aura of other people because our auras attract their body's electromagnetic waves into our electromagnetic field. The aura can be described as the atmosphere around an object or being that reflects its disposition or state of being to others. It combines all the energies flowing through you and communicates its general vibrational frequency. When people say a place has a bad vibe or that someone has a welcoming energy, they are actually sensing their aura.

The Energy Bodies of Your Aura

From a spiritual standpoint, your aura consists of various energy bodies and each emits its own energy. The combined effect of these energies is what other people feel as your aura.

The physical body is visually perceivable and allows you to function and exist in the physical plane. This body also houses the other imperceptible energy bodies.

The mental body stores your ideas, perceptions, beliefs, and feelings. It's where complex emotions and cognitive functions like reading, logic, and reason are processed and it powers your creativity and motivation.

The emotional body stores all your emotional impulses and the memory of any traumatic experiences you've had. Spiritualists believe the reptilian brain's stress response is coded into the human DNA. Because of this, the body remembers the trauma from past lives and instinctively tries to avoid similar experiences.

The spiritual body is where your higher self resides. Your higher self is what creates your conscious and subconscious minds and when these two are connected, you have access to your higher self. This is the eternal part of your being that remembers all your experiences from different lifetimes and has access to divine knowledge. Your higher self is connected to the universe so you can only access this part of your being when your vibrations are high and you have a raised consciousness.

When the energies in your aura are mostly light, you vibrate at a higher plane of consciousness and have a positive perspective on life. People resonate with this energy and react positively to your presence. This also enables you to attract and manifest more positivity into your life. Neutral energies give you the capacity to attract light energy and raise your vibrations. When the energies are mostly negative, your aura is dense and clogged up. No new energy can flow into and through you because the negative energy is stagnant. This is why it's so difficult to get out of a bad mood or to rid yourself of low frequency feelings and emotions. Energy attracts other energies that are in the same frequency range as itself so if you don't take conscious steps to release the negative energy, it will keep on growing.

Being Aware And Raising Your Vibrations

Every environment and person we encounter carries their own energy and our aura absorbs it whether we are conscious of it or not. For example, you may notice that eating certain foods, watching certain TV shows, or listening to certain music leaves you feeling heavy, dense, and lethargic but you don't put much thought into it. That's because we're always absorbing the energy from any stimuli we encounter through our senses. Unfortunately, modern lifestyles have desensitized us so much from our feelings and emotions it takes a concentrated effort on our part to become mindfully aware of them.

We must understand that light energy is dynamic and constantly moving, whereas negative energy is stagnant. This is why positive emotions seem so fleeting while negative emotions and moods seem to last longer, sometimes carrying on for months or years at a time. Human beings always synchronize their energy to the energy of their environment, in part because energy tends to resonate with other energies and also because our need to belong is part of our instinctive survival tactics. When your aura's frequency is low, your perspective of life is negative and you will only resonate with negative experiences and this cycle will continue until you consciously make the effort to break it. This is why mindfulness and awareness are the first steps towards evaluating the thoughts, feelings, and emotions weighing you down and then releasing them so you can raise your vibration.

The easiest way to become aware is to draw your focus into yourself in a moment of stillness. If you are doing this for the first few times, then it's best to start at night when there is limited external stimuli. You'll be able to feel the different energy bodies within you and begin to evaluate each one's frequency. Naturally, when you are new to this level of awareness, you will struggle to maintain your focus because your mind is so accustomed to filtering through multiple external stimuli at a time. You may find your thoughts wandering off to all the tasks you have to complete the next day or the video you watched right before you went to bed. You have to fight these intrusive thoughts off and the best way to do it is through meditation. Meditation helps you increase your awareness because it helps your mind focus on a single object, thought, or feeling and puts you in control of expanding that awareness as you see fit.

The Difference Between Awareness And Consciousness

Awareness and consciousness have different meanings despite being used interchangeably. Awareness happens when you take note of your internal and external state of being. You are aware of the interplay between your energy and the energies of other people and environments. Your awareness is limited to the things you can perceive with your physical sensory body.

Consciousness is a deeper and more spiritual kind of 'awareness'. When you're conscious, you are connected to your higher self and your understanding and perspective of life is not limited to what you can perceive with your physical body. Your higher self is a light frequency being, so being conscious means your vibrations are raised.

You can't be connected to your higher self if you're not aware of your physical being and the thoughts, emotions, and feelings lowering your vibrations in the first place. It therefore follows that awareness precedes consciousness. Understandably, these two terms are often used to mean the same thing because they are almost inextricably connected. When you are aware, you can intentionally release negative emotions and clear your aura of their negative energy. This creates the capacity for your aura to absorb light energy which raises your vibrations. When your vibrations are raised, your connection to your higher self strengthens and you're able to adopt a higher, more positive perspective on life. This happens even if you are facing a particularly challenging situation because your higher self's understanding is not limited to what you see or know in the physical plane. You need to consistently and intentionally increase your awareness and consciousness because light energy is always moving and it's easy to get stuck in the cycle of negativity again.

Raising Your Vibrations And Healing Your Energy Bodies

Raising your vibrations allows you to heal any ailments that have manifested themselves in your different energy bodies as a result of the dense negative energy you were carrying in your aura.

The Physical Body
When your vibrations are raised, the diseases caused by your stress response are alleviated. This includes improved circulation, sleeping patterns, digestion, and an increased heart rate.

The Mental Body
For the most part, the shift from a low frequency to a high frequency happens in the mind, probably because it also functions on the frequencies of your brainwaves. In any case, when your vibrations are raised, the release of negative thoughts and emotions means feelings of anxiety and depression no longer overwhelm you. You can think more

clearly and without the tint of negativity clouding your mind's eye. This helps you to rationalize your experiences from a neutral perspective and release trauma. You're able to focus your mind on the things you want and manifest positivity into your reality.

The Emotional Body

When your emotional body is healing, you have greater control over your emotional impulses and your relaxation response is more active than your stress response. This improves your emotional wellbeing because a lot of irrational and harmful behaviors are a result of the low vibrational emotions coming from trauma and the stress response.

The Spiritual Body

The well-being of the other energy bodies is mostly determined by the external stimuli you absorb and the energy of these stimuli attracts other energies of the same frequency. When you're vibrating at a higher frequency, you attract the abundance of other high frequency energies and you're able to manifest positivity into your life. You are also more connected to your higher self and have access to the knowledge of what you truly want and need. Your vibrations send these wants and needs out into the universe so they can be drawn towards you. This is how the law of attraction manifests things into your physical reality.

The Mind-Body-Spirit Connection

Before I explain this connection, I feel it's important I highlight the difference between the mind and the brain. The brain is the biological machinery allowing us to experience life through our thoughts, feelings, and emotions. The mind is the part of our being made up of these thoughts, feelings, and emotions. If these two were not connected, you would be able to put your hand on a hot stove and not feel the pain of your skin burning or learn to not put your hand on a hot stove in the future. This knowing and feeling is an integral part of the human experience. That's why some spiritualists say there is no mind-body connection because we're mind-body beings. They argue we cannot separate these two aspects and analyze them individually because to do so is to take away the very essence of what makes us human.

There's a third part of this connection that is often forgotten about, even in the spiritual world. The spirit is a key part of this connection because it is the life force or *prana* that makes the functioning of your body possible. I briefly discussed the mind-body-spirit connection earlier when I looked at the effects of negative emotions on the spiritual body. This connection is what interlinks your mental, emotional, and physical wellbeing. Unfortunately, science has only recently began proving the existence of this connection so the research on the topic is scant at best. Of the few studies that exist, some found terminally ill patients who believed they were going to die were less likely to survive. Likewise, patients who were badly injured but believed they were going to make a full recovery were observed to heal at a faster rate than those who were unsure of their recovery. It seems the key here is in what you feel and believe to be true. The brain is incapable of differentiating your thoughts and feelings from the physical reality in the same way that it's incapable of differentiating a real threat from a perceived one. This means when you think and believe a certain thing to be true, your body's vibrations align themselves with this. This alters the vibrations of your brain waves and cells and they too begin to operate accordingly. Our emotions, beliefs, and feelings create our thoughts and determine our vibrations. When our vibrations are low, there's a misalignment in the mind-body-spirit connection and this manifests itself in illness in the various energy bodies as a signal that something is off kilter. In contrast, when our vibrations are high, all the energy in our aura is aligned and there is no lack in any of our energy bodies.

You now have a deeper understanding of how energy affects your emotional, physical, and mental wellbeing from a spiritual perspective. When you combine the knowledge contained in these two chapters, you can form a holistic picture of how emotions and energies work together to create what we know to be a beautifully complex human experience. Now that you have all this knowledge, you need practical information on how to release negative emotions and clear away their energy so you can come into a positive state of mind.

Chapter 3: Sound Therapy

You've learnt that energy is generally intangible and imperceivable to humans. Sound is produced when energy vibrates at a frequency our ears can perceive. What we hear is created when the waves of its vibrations crash into each other through a medium such as water, air, or a table. The speed of the sound waves depends on the space between the molecules of the medium concerned. Sound moves the fastest when it's transferred through a solid medium because the particles of a solid are very close to each other. This is why we can touch solid items like tables, doors, and cellphones. The molecules of a liquid are further apart so the sound waves will slow down when they pass through water for example. Sound travels at its slowest in gases because their molecules are so far apart we can barely see it with the naked eye. When sound energy enters the ear canal, it converts to electrical energy so the nerves can convey it to the brain through electrical impulses. Sounds can alter brain waves to elicit a specific emotional response when they are converted to electrical energy because all external stimuli is processed by the brain through electrical signals.

Sound plays an important role in our lives and we see its effects everyday, though we may not be aware of it. Think of the kinds of sounds played in a horror movie or on commercials. Each of these has instantly recognizable sounds, even if you're not watching the movie or commercial. You can identify a horror movie by listening to its audio because the bone-chilling screams and the suspenseful sounds elicit a certain reaction out of you. Even musicians who are hearing impaired are able to compose the most beautiful melodies. They can 'hear' the music through its frequencies and are able to identify different pitches based on how they feel the soundwaves in their bodies.

Furthermore, humans naturally attach emotions to sound either by associating them with certain memories or using them to express/generate specific emotions. For example, when you're frustrated you grunt and when you're relieved you sigh. This is why people have 'feel good' songs that can lift their moods and put them in high spirits. This phenomenon has been backed by science, with one study finding that listening to pleasant sounds releases the pleasure hormone called dopamine (Salimpoor *et al*, 2011). Another study from the University of Pennsylvania's School of Medicine found our emotions can affect how we perceive sound and vice versa (Zupan et al, 2014). If you experienced a traumatic event while a certain song was playing, then hearing any song with a similar melody will trigger the memory of that event and the emotions associated with it. This happens even if the sound is one you previously found to be pleasant because trauma changed how you perceive it.

This is the power of sound therapy. It affects your mind-body-spirit connection both consciously and unconsciously. Considering that sound is present in every single moment of our lives, it's wise to learn how you can manipulate those frequencies to help you move into a positive state of mind.

What Is Sound Therapy?

Sound therapy is the use of sound waves accompanied by mindfulness to improve your spiritual, emotional, and physical health. Ancient civilizations have long used sounds as a means to heal their physical beings and connect to the universe. Rituals and practices across the spiritual spectrum have always included clapping, singing, playing instruments and chanting as a way to facilitate the connection and healing. Sound therapy is a method that intentionally converts negative frequencies in your body into positive ones by synchronizing them with the light frequencies of sound energy. It also helps control your body's physiological response to stressors and curbs the illnesses caused by an overactive stress response. This occurs because sound stimulates the parts of the brain controlling emotional impulses and hormone secretions. For example, a pleasant sound can signal your brain to secrete oxytocin which relieves pain and makes you feel happy and relaxed.

Sound is one of the ways in which our senses gather information to be sent to the brain and forms an important part in memory formation, especially during the "fight, flight or freeze" response. When you use sound to release negative emotions you can manipulate the brain into restraining your overactive stress response. The long term effect of this is the brain becomes rewired to trigger a relaxation response over memories where it previously went into stress mode.

How Does it Work?

Sound therapy primarily works on the phenomena of resonance and entrainment. Resonance occurs when an object emits a frequency onto another object and causes it to vibrate at the same frequency as itself. Our bodies are mostly made of water and this allows the soundwaves to travel faster than they would in air.

Entrainment occurs when two objects of different frequencies influence each other's frequencies until they synchronize. Both these phenomena result in two objects harmonizing and vibrating at the same frequency. This happens either due to one object lowering or increasing its frequency or both objects meeting in the middle to create a new, mutual frequency.

Sound therapy is most effective when used in tandem with mindfulness methods such as meditation. This helps to increase your awareness and focus your energy on fully absorbing the soundwaves and the intentions behind them. The awareness also helps facilitate your ascension to a higher consciousness where you can connect with your higher self. If you're using sound therapy to help you with an emotion you are struggling to get rid of, then connecting to your higher self will give you access to new knowledge and a fresh perspective on the cause of the emotion and what you need to do to release it. This is sometimes the case when an emotion is caused by a situation we're trying to avoid because it makes us uncomfortable or we're not sure how to handle it.

The ultimate goal of sound therapy is to bring balance to all the frequencies of the different energy bodies. Although you can use any sound frequency to facilitate the release of negative emotions, the most effective way to do sound therapy is to listen to sounds consisting purely of the sacred frequencies used for spiritual healing for centuries.

Sounds That Affect Brain Waves

While all sounds can affect our emotions, some have been shown to have a greater effect than others.

Subliminals are sounds usually containing hidden messages aimed at influencing our emotions and go straight to the subconscious mind. These sounds contain affirmations at a frequency we cannot hear, allowing them to bypass the conscious mind.

Solfeggio sounds are high frequency sounds consisting of six tones, each with a specific effect on our brainwaves.

Binaural sounds use entrainment by exposing each ear to a different frequency, creating a third harmonized frequency that affects our brainwaves.

Isochronic tones are audible single frequency sounds creating a pulsating beat by being turned on and off at regular intervals. They are usually a background sound, accompanying binaural beats or Solfeggio chants.

Benefits of Sound Therapy

Sound therapy combats negative emotions and its effects on the body. When you release trapped emotions, your disposition improves from one of stress and anxiety to one of peace, harmony, and balances your energy by removing energy blockages. Sound therapy helps you control your body's stress response which in turn lowers your blood pressure, regulates your breathing, and improves your circulation and sleep patterns. The sounds signal the body's response and build the body's resilience against stressors.

From a spiritual standpoint, sound therapy helps to raise your vibrations and remove the blockages caused by the negative energy previously trapped in your aura. The mindfulness required enhances your awareness and facilitates your connection with your higher self. Even if you don't explicitly include affirmations as part of your sound therapy sessions, the intention you have while practicing them will affect your frequency.

Types Of Sound Therapy

Listening To Or Creating Music

Singing, humming, listening, or creating music can improve your mood and evoke positive emotions. If you want to combat and release a negative emotion, you can listen to or create music. The sound will usually have a higher frequency, forcing the negative emotion to increase its frequency and synchronize with the music's frequency. Prolonged exposure to music can improve memory retention as shown by studies on the effects of classical music on our ability to learn. The studies found that the music of composers like Beethoven, Mozart, and Chopin enhances child development and increases brain activity (Jenkins, 2001).

Drumming is one of the best ways to release negative energy, especially when done in a group. The unique rhythmic sounds of drums awaken feelings of joy, love, and compassion within the drummer and the rapid arm movements needed to play the instrument help to shake negative energy out of your body. The music of the drums also encourages people to dance and move their bodies as another way of releasing stagnant energy. The great thing about drums is you can play them alone, with other people, or you could simply be present and absorb the frequencies. Some spiritualists have suggested the reason why drums are such an effective sound therapy tool is because they mimic the sounds of a beating heart.

Music has been found to reduce cortisol levels in the bloodstream and aid the secretion of dopamine. This reduces feelings of depression and anxiety and helps you feel relaxed. Finally, most people feel the need to move their bodies when they listen to music and this encourages the flow of energy and makes it easier for negative energy to be released from the body.

Guided Meditation

This meditation uses audio recordings to guide you through this mindful practice. During guided meditation, you focus on the sound of the instructor's voice as they guide you through various activities and visualizations. These can include positive affirmations or recalling happy memories. You could also be asked to think of a situation that is currently causing you distress and think of positive ways you can handle it, thus changing your perspective on it. You can follow guided meditations for free through apps and other media platforms.

Binaural Beats

As I mentioned above, binaural tones occur when each ear is exposed to a slightly different frequency with a combined frequency lower than 1000 Hz. The reptilian brain hears and interprets the third harmonized frequency (the binaural beat). The binaural beat is often less than 30 Hz, which is the same frequency range that brainwaves operate within. Binaural sounds stimulate each of the five brainwave frequencies naturally occurring in the mind. These brain waves are Delta, Theta, Alpha, Beta, and Gamma in order of ascending frequency. The irregular functioning of any of these waves due to the lowered frequency of negative emotions can cause serious health issues.

- **Delta-** 0-4 Hz. Binaural beats in this range improve your sleep and make you feel more relaxed.

- **Theta-** 4-8 Hz. This range improves your creativity and intuition, allowing you to have a stronger connection with your higher self and raised consciousness.

- **Alpha-** 8-12 Hz. This range promotes positive thinking and long term relaxation.

- **Beta-** 12-40 Hz. These waves are most prominent in the neocortex and binaural beats in this range contribute to improved cognitive functions such as reading, logic, and speech.

Solfeggio Frequencies

Solfeggio frequencies were first used in Gregorian music during the 9th century and can be incorporated into music or chants. These high frequency chants encourage a balanced mind by synchronizing brainwaves to their vibrations. These frequencies were rediscovered by Dr Joseph Puleo during the 1970s and he began conducting research on them. Unlike binaural beats, Solfeggio frequencies consist of a single frequency that resonates with our brainwaves. They historically consist of a six tone scale with the following effects:

- **396 Hz** is associated with freeing you from feelings of fear and guilt.

- **417 Hz** encourages change as it's been found to slow down heart rates. This alleviates the brain from its automatic response to past trauma.

- **528 Hz** is known in the spiritual community for facilitating miracles. Scientifically, it aids in repairing DNA by changing the reptilian brain's genetically coded emotional impulses. This was proven by a study conducted in 1988 by Dr. Glenn Rein who observed that DNA vials exposed to music with this frequency absorbed UV light much faster than those exposed to other frequencies (Rein, 1988). DNA's rate of UV light absorption indicates how healthy it is.

- **639 Hz** stimulates the parts of your brain dealing with connection and prompts you to heal your relationships with others.

- **741 Hz** affects the neocortex so it improves our problem-solving and logic skills. It encourages you to share your thoughts without the fear of rejection.

- **852 Hz** is known to help deepen our connection with your higher selves and the universe by helping you understand the divine order of everything in existence.

During his research, Dr Puleo discovered each note in the scale is aligned with the universal's numerical patterns and could be extrapolated according to the principles of mathematics and sacred geometry. When he did this, he uncovered three new Solfeggio frequencies:

- **174 Hz** which stimulates the brain into secreting the pain hormone oxytocin.

- **285 Hz** which is known to help accelerate wound healing.

- **963 Hz** which induces a spiritual awakening.

Mantras And Affirmations as Vocal Toning

Mantras are a great sound therapy technique because the vibrations of your voice carry the energy of words into our surroundings. While you can say your mantras and affirmations using 'the mind's voice', it's more effective to vocalize them because this bypasses the brain's rationalization of your words and speeds up the physical manifestation of their energy. Most people are socialized to react to negative emotions with a desire to change themselves when these emotions are meant to draw their attention towards a change in the environment that requires fixing. Mantras and affirmations help you to respond to negative emotions in the latter by increasing your self-compassion. They help you focus on one thing at a time by shutting out other external stimuli and creating space for your mind to process and release negative emotions. A 2012 study published in the *Journal for Alternative and Complementary Medicine* recorded the effects of meditation on people who suffered from anxiety and memory loss. It found that the patients had increased memory retention and reduced levels of anxiety after partaking in an eight week meditation program (Moss *et al*, 2012).

Some of the most popular and most effective mantras come from chakra meditation. Our minds are naturally inclined to voice our emotions in single syllable frequencies. A baby's first vocalizations are often a repetition of single syllable sounds such as da da. The ancient Hindu practice of chakra meditation uses this principle in their single syllable mantras. Each mantra is connected to a different chakra and has a specific effect on the body. According to Hindu and Buddist philosophy, chakras are the centres of energy located along the body, starting from the base of your spine to the crown of your head. Energy flows freely through the body when the chakras are balanced. There are seven chakras and each functions as follows:

- The **Root chakra** is located at the base of the spine and is linked to your need for security, belonging, and your basic survival needs. The LAM mantra unblocks this chakra and allows you to feel safe. This chakra is associated with the color red.

- The **Sacral chakra** is found below the navel and controls your sense of pleasure and creativity. The VAM mantra strengthens your connection with your higher self. This chakra is orange in color.

- The **Solar Plexus chakra** is around the stomach and powers your sense of motivation and self-will. When this chakra is unblocked by the RAM mantra, you trust yourself more. This is the yellow chakra.

- The **Heart chakra** is situated in the heart and controls your ability to connect with others with a spirit of love, compassion, and forgiveness. The LAM mantra enables you to interact with people from a place of calm and understanding. This chakra is identified with the color green.

- The **Throat chakra** is found in the throat and powers communication, honesty, and authenticity. When this chakra is activated using the HAM mantra, you can effectively and confidently articulate yourself. This chakra is blue.

- The **Third Eye chakra** is located on the forehead, just above the eyes and is where you receive sacred wisdom and understanding of your highest self and the universe. This chakra is unlocked with the OM mantra which increases your intuition and sharpens your vision. This is the purple chakra.

- The **Crown chakra** is at the top of your head and signifies a complete connection with your higher self and the universe. This chakra is also unlocked with the OM mantra. It's associated with white to symbolize the complete unity of self.

Each chakra can be identified with a color that best symbolizes it. These colors are assigned in the order of their frequencies and that's why the Heart chakra is assigned the color green instead of red. Red has a lower frequency than green. These colors can also help you focus on the chakra you're trying to clear during your meditation. Visualization is one of the strongest tools for mindfulness because it activates the mind's eye. You intensify the intention to raise your vibrations by consistently visualizing your desires. For example, if you want to unlock your creativity, you can imagine yourself painting in a studio, singing on-stage or doing whatever you imagine your creative haven looking like. This helps you manifest your wants into the physical world.

Singing Bowls

Singing bowls create a strong sound triggering the body's relaxation response by harmonizing its frequency with your brain waves. Traditionally, these bowls are made of metals or metal alloys and originate from the Himalayan area. However, some singing bowls are made out of quartz sand and have a clear or opaque appearance. Each bowl has a different frequency, depending on its size and the material it's made of. Research suggests the frequency from these bowls induces relaxation by stimulating the brain's alpha brainwaves.

The frequency of the metal bowls harmonize the theta and alpha brainwaves. The combined effect of this is a stronger connection to your higher self and the stimulation of your brain's relaxation response. Some metal bowls produce sounds resembling the OM mantra used to activate the Third Eye and Crown chakras. These bowls are ideal if you want to experience a sound bath that puts you in a generally relaxed, almost sleep-like state.

Crystal singing bowls are especially powerful because of the material they're made out of. Quartz is a crystal and crystals have their own magnetic fields and can act as amplifiers of energy. If you set an intention as you play the crystal bowl, it will be magnified in the soundwaves. These bowls are great for the targeted unblocking of specific chakras because you can set your intention to heal or activate the areas controlled by that chakra. For example, if you are having a hard time forgiving someone, you can set your intention towards channeling the Heart chakra. You may even place a green light inside the bowl to further amplify this intention.

Some say the best result comes from using both bowls to help raise your vibrations. You can start off with the metal bowl which lulls you into a relaxed state and connects you with your higher self. You can then transition to the crystal bowl to help you manifest a specific outcome.

You should take care to set intentions that are aligned with your true wants and needs. Crystals are what is known as a one dimensional object, meaning they have no awareness of anything beyond their existence. They only resonate with your aura's frequency and amplify this into the brain. So you need to make sure the intentions you set are a true reflection of what you feel and think before you accidentally find yourself on the business end of the law of attraction.

Gong Baths

Gongs are large percussion instruments almost resembling a cymbal. They are usually made out of metals like bronze and are hung up on walls or mounted onto frames. These instruments produce very powerful high frequency sounds and each one makes a different sound, depending on its size. Gong baths are most effective when you lie down and let someone stroke the gong while you close your eyes and let the sound wash over you.

Tuning Forks

Tuning forks are the perfect example of how resonance is used to heal the body and release energy. They are typically used by musicians to tune their instruments. The musician will strike the fork and then continue to tune their instrument until it resonates with the pitch given off. Similarly, you can have someone strike a tuning fork and then place it close to your body. After some time, your body will resonate with the frequency being emitted by the fork. It's more effective to ask a skilled practitioner or at least someone with musical knowledge to strike the fork for you or to teach you how to use it if you want your body to vibrate at a specific frequency.

All of these methods work in varied ways and some can be practiced alone while others require the assistance of an experienced practitioner or just another person to help you with the logistics thereof. You can use one or more of them as you see fit to heal your body and raise your vibrations.

Chapter 4: Breathwork

Breathing is one of the body's most essential functions and it generally happens unconsciously. The brain cannot survive without oxygen and once the brain dies, all bodily functions slowly start to shut down. Breathing powers the body in both a physical and spiritual sense.

Breathwork is the practice of consciously controlling your breathing patterns to nourish the body and facilitate the release of toxins and dense energy. Both Chinese and Hindu spiritual philosophies believe breathing oxygen is how energy enters and leaves the body. This energy is your life force and is known as *qi* or *prana* and its flow in your body is inhibited when your aura is filled with dense, negative energy. Both philosophies believe our shallow breathing encourages low energy because it doesn't sufficiently facilitate the release of negative energy. Breathwork requires deep breaths and facilitates the release of negative energy from your aura while nourishing your nervous system. Most breathwork techniques typically involve an alternation between shallow, rapid breaths and deep, slow ones.

Scientifically, breathing places oxygen into the bloodstream which then flows around the body, oxygenating the organs. The oxygen you inhale combines with glucose from the food in your stomach to create adenosine triphosphate or ATP. In a nutshell, ATP powers every cell in your body and without it, the body has no energy to power any of its functions. When you respire, you inhale the oxygen from the atmosphere and exhale the carbon dioxide produced by your cells as they break food down in your body. Having too much carbon dioxide in your body slows it down because it replaces oxygen. Breathing also directly affects your heart rate as your heart rate increases when you inhale oxygen and decreases when you exhale carbon dioxide.

Breathwork increases your self-awareness and releases toxins and negative energy from the body. It also decreases your stress levels and alleviates the ailments associated with an overactive stress response (muscle tension, anxiety, digestive problems, memory loss etc.)

The long term benefits include an expanded lung capacity and increased lung strength, higher energy levels and improved immunity.

Different Breathwork Techniques

Breathwork focuses your attention on your breathing so it increases your self-awareness. Because of this, it's often used in tandem with meditation, yoga, and other mindful practices. It can also be accompanied by sound therapy techniques like mantras and singing bowls. All the techniques require you to have a straight and relaxed spine so the oxygen can flow through your entire body. You can achieve this by sitting upright or laying flat on your back with raised knees and feet planted on the floor. It's important to begin each technique in a physically relaxed state. You need to unclench the jaws, relax your facial muscles, and roll your shoulders backwards and down (be careful not to slump them as this contracts the spine).

It's important that you start small because if you overexert yourself at the first few tries, you may seriously harm yourself and cause unnecessary damage to your body. If you have health complications and are unsure whether you can do breathwork, then you should contact a doctor. Generally, breathwork is not advised for people who have a family history of aneurysms, seizures or epileptic attacks. You should also steer away from it if you have heart diseases, are prone to strokes or if you've recently had surgery.

Rhythmic Breathing

Rhythmic breathing is the easiest technique to try if you are new to breathwork. It gently helps you transition from consciously taking note of your natural breathing pattern to taking deeper breaths. For the first cycle or two, simply observe your natural pattern and count the length of your inhales and exhales. After this, you can count your breath in four parts:

- inhale for three counts
- hold your breath for two counts
- exhale for three counts
- hold your breath for two counts

You can gradually increase the number of cycles as your body becomes comfortable with the pattern. After this, you can try a ratio that induces deeper breaths like the 4-7-8 method. With this method you must:

- inhale for four counts through the nose
- hold your breath for seven counts
- exhale for eight counts

Once again, you can increase the number of cycles according to your comfortability level.

These two techniques of breathwork are the best ones for beginners because they gently introduce your body to taking deeper breaths and breath retention without requiring you to overexert yourself.

Alternate Nostril Breathing

This breathwork technique is known in Sanskrit as *Nadi Shodhana* and requires you to breathe through one nostril at a time, alternating between them in equal ratios. To begin, take your right hand and place the index and middle fingers on your forehead, focussing your concentration to the Third Eye chakra. Your ring finger will be positioned next to your left nostril and the thumb will be next to your right nostril.

- Start by inhaling through both nostrils and immediately closing them at the top of the breath
- Open the right nostril and exhale
- Inhale through the right nostril and plug it with the thumb at the top of the breath
- Open the left nostril and exhale
- Inhale through the left nostril and plug it with the ring finger at the top of the breath

You can repeat this cycle as many times as you can and once you're comfortable, you can hold your breath in between each inhale and exhale.

It doesn't matter which nostril you exhale out of first, as long as you inhale through the same nostril you just exhaled from. The point of breathwork is to increase your body's oxygen intake so you gradually increase the depth of your breath until each inhale fills the lungs to its fullest capacity and each exhale completely empties the lungs.

Breath of Fire

Breath of Fire is commonly used during Kundalini Yoga to activate all seven chakras and allow the Kundalini life force to flow through the body. It includes rapid nasal breathing powered by the Solar Plexus chakra. The navel is used to pump energy up along the body on the exhale by pushing it towards the spine when you breathe out and relaxing the stomach (pushing the navel forward) when you inhale.

- You can begin by sitting crossed-legged with your hands comfortably placed on your knees.
- The hands are traditionally placed in the *Gyan mudra,* a hand posture where the index finger and thumb are touching.
- Rapidly breath in and out without pauses in between, making sure each inhale and exhale are of equal length and depth.
- You can place your hands on your navel to help you activate the Solar Plexus chakra.
- Repeat this cycle as much as you can without stopping.
- To finish, take a deep breath and relax your hands before allowing your breathing pattern to return to its natural rhythm.

You will notice your breaths are not as deep when you begin because your lungs are not used to taking rapid and deep breaths at the same time. You can train your lungs by breaking the method down to help you master the technique. You can start by panting as if hyperventilating and then gradually taking deeper breaths as time goes on or you can start by taking deep breaths and gradually decreasing the length of each breath until you are breathing rapidly. Once you've mastered the breathing part, you can focus on engaging your core muscles as you pump through the navel.

Holotropic Breathwork

This technique was developed in the 1970s by Stanislav and Christina Grof as a healing tool during therapy. Like Breath of Fire, this technique can induce an altered state of consciousness because of the change in oxygen and carbon dioxide concentration in the lungs caused by the rapid breaths. Holotropic breathwork is fully immersive and requires teamwork so it needs to be facilitated by a trained practitioner. One session can last for a few minutes or a few hours and incorporates music, bodywork, and artistic expression. Each session is conducted in groups, with people being paired together as 'breathers' and 'sitters'.

- The 'breather' lies down and closes their eyes, focusing on being present in the moment. The 'sitter' is only there to ensure the 'breather' follows instructions and for emotional support.
- The practitioner will then play soothing music that evokes memories and feelings from the 'breather'. These are usually past traumas at the root of the breather's toxic behaviors and mood disorders.
- They are instructed to take deep, successive breaths into the navel. As the session progresses, the practitioner will instruct the breathers to increase the depth and length of their breathing until it's rapid and continuous.

- At this point, the breather's negative emotions have been brought to the fore and the practitioner will instruct them to intuitively express these. They can kick, scream or make any other sounds and movements.

After this, they will be given tools to creatively express their experience and are encouraged to speak about it within their groups. The creative outlet may vary in each session. In some sessions, the participants will also take part in bodywork such as reiki, yoga or acupuncture to help release the negative energy from their bodies. In the following session, the 'sitter' and 'breather' will switch roles and the process starts again.

The technique is effective because your stress response is most alert when you are lying down as this is the most vulnerable position you can be in. The evocative music brings all your negative emotions to the fore and you are allowed to express them as you would during a real threat. Creatively expressing these emotions helps you connect with your higher self and allows you to loosen the mental grip these emotions have on you because your higher self is a being of bliss and peace. Talking through your experience afterwards helps you view your behavior and emotions in a logical and reasonable way and the body work helps you to physically move that energy out of your body.

The disadvantage to holotropic breathwork is you may not be willing to pay for a breathwork session or you may be uncomfortable with having such a personal experience in front of many people. I'd venture to say that this technique is more suited for people with extroverted personalities as they are known to draw energy from external sources more than introverts do.

Techniques that are meant to raise your vibrations require a component of meditative mindfulness to put yourself into a state of awareness. Luckily, breathwork itself is a state of awareness because it's entire purpose is to make you focus on one thing: your breathing. Some breathwork techniques provide an easier way to raise your vibrations because you don't need any instrument, audio tracks, or tools to facilitate the process. All you need is yourself and a comfortable and solid base to sit or lie down on.

Conclusion

This book was created to provide the reader with a comprehensive and easily digestible understanding of how you can raise your vibrations and to convert skeptics of spiritual practices by showing how science has begun proving the ancient spiritual truths spiritualists have known since time immemorial.

To begin, I provided an in-depth explanation of why we have emotions, how they come to be in our minds and how we express them to the world at large. This was followed by a breakdown of the brain's structure so you could understand how external stimuli become behaviors and emotions through the use of biological machinery. This included a breakdown of how each part of the brain controls different parts of the body and how these differences come into play based on the emotions being experienced. Then I set out the differences between moods, feelings, and emotions. I then laid out how emotions physiologically and spiritually affect us before closing off with an explanation of the law of resonance and how we can perpetuate our emotions beyond ourselves and become stuck in a loop of negative emotions.

The second chapter provided you with a clear understanding of the mechanics of energy and how our auras are an amalgamation of the different energies we absorb and subsequently emit. I explained how raising your vibrations works and how an imbalance in one part of your being affects every part. This section included examples of how one energy body helps heal or hinder the other. This chapter ended with an explanation of the principles of the law of attraction and an example of how science has been able to prove, to a small degree, what you think affects how your body functions.

From here on, I gave examples of different breathwork and sound therapy techniques you can use to raise your vibrations and release negative energy from your body. Some of these require instruments and tools while others need you to be part of a group or have someone helping you. I provided a step-by-step breakdown of how you can easily apply any number of these techniques to your life today. But there are a few you can do alone in the comfort of your home if you're uncomfortable with the idea of having such an intimate experience in the presence of other people.

With this book in hand, you can start your journey towards a better, more emotionally balanced life today. All you need to do is take the first step and the rest will fall into place. In fact, you already took the first step by reading through the book and now all you have to do is keep that momentum going. You can put this book down and listen to some soothing music or take slow deep breaths as a first step. It's as simple as that.

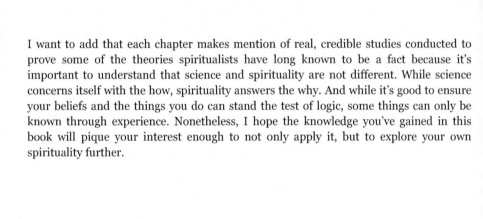

I want to add that each chapter makes mention of real, credible studies conducted to prove some of the theories spiritualists have long known to be a fact because it's important to understand that science and spirituality are not different. While science concerns itself with the how, spirituality answers the why. And while it's good to ensure your beliefs and the things you do can stand the test of logic, some things can only be known through experience. Nonetheless, I hope the knowledge you've gained in this book will pique your interest enough to not only apply it, but to explore your own spirituality further.

References

Admin. (2014 August 26). How to Use Toning & Breath for Meditation. *Soundings of the Planet: Instrumental New Age Relaxation Music & Nature Sounds for Meditation, Yoga, Massage, Spas.* soundings.com/what-is-vocal-toning-anyway/.

Alex. (2020 August 9). The Mind-Body Connection Explained. *The Supplemental Magazine.* blog.vitally.com/mind-body-connection-explained.

AstroYogi. (2020). Chakra Meditation - Most Significant Benefits of Chakra Meditation. *Astro Yogi.* www.astroyogi.com/meditation/chakra.

BD Editors. (2017 April 28). Adenosine Triphosphate (ATP) - Definition, Structure and Functions. *Biology Dictionary.* biologydictionary.net/atp/.

Bernardi, L. (2005 December 9). Cardiovascular, Cerebrovascular, and Respiratory Changes Induced by Different Types of Music in Musicians and Non-Musicians: The Importance of Silence. *Heart,*(4), 445–452.

Brogaard, Berit. (2018) Basic and Complex Emotions. *Psychology Today.* www.psychologytoday.com/us/blog/the-superhuman-mind/201806/basic-and-complex-emotions.

Carne, Sharon. (2019 March 16). What Is the Difference between Tibetan and Crystal Singing Bowls? *Sound Wellness.* soundwellness.com/tibetan-crystal-singing-bowls/.

Cherry, Kendra. (2013 August 2). Emotions and Types of Emotional Responses. *Verywell Mind.* www.verywellmind.com/what-are-emotions-2795178.

Chia, Debbie. (2017 April 8). The Esoteric Art of Healing through Sonic Vibrations and Beyond. *Meoko.* meoko.net/the-esoteric-art-of-healing-through-sonic-vibrations-and-beyond/.

Cronkleton, Emily. (2017 October 6). Holotropic Breathwork: Usage, Safety, and More. *Healthline.* www.healthline.com/health/holotropic-breathwork.

Daily Life Staff. (2020 August 22).Why You Need to Practice the Breath of Fire Daily. *Daily Life.* dailylife.com/article/breath-of-fire#:~:text=%20Here%20is%20how%20to%20do%20the%20breath.

Desy, Phylameana. (2019 May 9). Learn about the 5 Layers of Energy Surrounding Your Physical Body. *Learn Religions.* www.learnreligions.com/layers-of-human-energy-field-1729677.

Detyna, Danuta. (2016 October 14). The Damage of Fight or Flight and What to Do about It. *HoneyColony.* www.honeycolony.com/article/fight-or-flight/.

Dimas, Jessica. (2020 February 11). How to Heal the Mind-Body-Spirit Connection. *Dwell in Magic*. jessicadimas.com/mind-body-spirit/.

Ericson, John. (2013 June 30). Fundamental Link between Emotions and Sound Perception Identified in New Study. *Medical Daily*. www.medicaldaily.com/fundamental-link-between-emotions-and-sound-perception-identified-new-study-247281.

Everyday Power Staff. (2020 October 26). Feelings Quotes on the Importance of Understanding Your Emotions. *Everyday Power*. everydaypower.com/feelings-quotes/#:~:text=Feeling%20Quotes%20About%20The%20Beauty%20Of%20Emotions.%20l.

FeelDoppel.com. (2019 March 19). What Is Entrainment and How Does the Human Body Respond to Rhythm? *Doppel*. 19 March 2019. feeldoppel.com/blogs/news/what-is-entrainment-and-how-does-the-human-body-respond-to-rhythm.

Fletcher, Jenna. 4-7-8 Breathing: How It Works, Benefits, and Uses. *Medical News Today*. Www.medicalnewstoday.com. www.medicalnewstoday.com/articles/324417.

Freedman, Joshua. (2018 August 16). What's the Difference between Emotion, Feeling, Mood? *Six Seconds*. www.6seconds.org/2017/05/15/emotion-feeling-mood/.

Freshwater, Shawna. (2017 May 11). Understanding Emotions. *Shawna Freshwater, PhD*. spacioustherapy.com/understanding-emotions/#:~:text=The%20word%20emotion%20comes%20from%20%E2%80%9Cmotion%E2%80%9D%20movement.%20All.

G, Rahul. (2019 June 29). Mantra Meditation — the Why, the How, and the Methods. *Medium*. medium.com/@rahul.goyl/mantra-meditation-the-why-the-how-and-the-methods-e71e58de6a3b.

Goleman, Daniel. (2007). *Emotional Intelligence*. Bantam Books.

Harper, Dylan. (2021 July 31). What Is the Difference between Awareness and Consciousness?. *Shift Frequency*. www.shiftfrequency.com/consciousness-vs-awareness-whats-the-big-difference/.

Hersh, Erica. (2020 November 3). Dangers of Singing Bowls: Myths and Potential Side Effects. *Healthline*. www.healthline.com/health/dangers-of-singing-bowls#What-is-singing-bowl-therapy?.

Jack, Rachael E, et al. (2014) Dynamic Facial Expressions of Emotion Transmit: An Evolving Hierarchy of Signals over Time. *Current Biology*,(2), 187-192.

Jenkins, J. S. (2001). The Mozart effect. *Journal of the Royal Society of Medicine*,(4), 170–172.

Kathy. (2016 November 19). Auras and Vibrational Energy. *Magnetic Law of Attraction.* magneticlawofattraction.com/auras-vibrational-energy/.

Kruizinga, Hendrik. (2016 June 16). Your 5 Brainwaves: Delta, Theta, Alpha, Beta and Gamma. *Lucid.* lucid.me/blog/5-brainwaves-delta-theta-alpha-beta-gamma/.

Kučera, Ondřej, and Daniel Havelka. (2012). Mechano-Electrical Vibrations of Microtubules--Link to Subcellular Morphology. *Bio Systems,*(3), 346–355.

Littrell, Jill. (2008). The Mind-Body Connection. *Social Work in Health Care,*(4), 17–37.

Mayo Clinic Staff. (2019 March 19). Chronic Stress Puts Your Health at Risk. *Mayo Clinic.* Mayo Foundation for Medical Education and Research. www.mayoclinic.org/healthy-lifestyle/stress-management/in-depth/stress/art-20046037.

Miller, Tanja, and Laila Nielsen. (2015). Measure of Significance of Holotropic Breathwork in the Development of Self-Awareness. *The Journal of Alternative and Complementary Medicine,*(12), 796–803.

Mind Vibrations Staff. (2019).Solfeggio Frequencies Guide: The Ancient Scale. *MindVibrations.* www.mindvibrations.com/solfeggio-frequencies/.

Moss, Aleezé Sattar, et al. (2012). Effects of an 8 Week Meditation Program on Mood and Anxiety in Patients with Memory Loss. *The Journal of Alternative and Complementary Medicine,*(1), 48–53.

Nyabuto, Dominic. (2020 March 5). Difference between Feelings, Emotions and Mood. *Dominic Nyabuto.* dominicnyabuto.com/difference-between-feelings-emotions-and-mood/.

Okter, Adnan. (2019). An Interesting Property of Water. *Evidence of Creation.* evidencesofcreation.wordpress.com/tag/how-do-we-perceive-matter/.

Olsgard, Meghan. (2017 September 27). Negative Emotions & Law of Attraction - They Aren't as Bad as You Might Think. *Infinite Soul Blueprint.* www.infinitesoulblueprint.com/law-of-attraction-negative-emotions/.

Palmer, Zandra. (2018 May 31). What Is Breathwork and Does It Work? A Doctor Explains the Science. *Parsley Health.* www.parsleyhealth.com/blog/breathwork-does-it-work/.

Parker, Chris A. (2021 February 18). "What Happens When You Raise Your Vibration?" *Light Warriors Legion.* lightwarriorslegion.com/what-happens-when-you-raise-your-vibration/.

Raypole, Crystal. (2020 August 18). Mantra Meditation: Benefits, How to Try It, and More. *Healthline.* www.healthline.com/health/mantra-meditation.

Relax Melodies. (n.d). The Science behind Solfeggio Frequencies. *Relax Melodies*. www.relaxmelodies.com/blog/science-behind-solfeggio-frequencies/.

Rodriguez, Steve. (2020 November 24). Resonance & Entrainment: Its Role in Energetic Healing. *Rico Torres World*. ricotorresworld.com/resonance-entrainment-its-role-in-energetic-healing/.

Salimpoor, V, et al. (2011). Anatomically distinct dopamine release during anticipation and experience of peak emotion to music. *Nature Neuroscience*,(4),257-262.

Santos-Longhurst, Adrienne. (2018). Sound Healing 101: What Is It and How Does It Work? *Healthline*. www.healthline.com/health/sound-healing.

Seastrunk, Byron. (2014 October 10). The Law of Resonance. *Opinion by Pen*. opinionbypen.com/law-resonance/.

Seladi-Schulman, Jill. (2018 July 23). What Part of the Brain Controls Emotions? Fear, Happiness, Anger, Love. *Healthline*. www.healthline.com/health/what-part-of-the-brain-controls-emotions#love.

Shah, Sejal. (2020 September 11). Alternate Nostril Breathing (Nadi Shodhana Pranayama). *Art of Living*. www.artofliving.org/us-en/yoga/breathing-techniques/alternate-nostril-breathing-nadi-shodhan.

Shahani, Kavita. (2020 April 11). Energy Clearing | How to Clear Negative Energy. *TheMindFool - Perfect Medium for Self-Development & Mental Health. Explorer of Lifestyle Choices & Seeker of the Spiritual Journey*. themindfool.com/energy-clearing/#:~:text=Energy%20clearing%20is%20not%20a%20process%20restric ted%20to.

Smith, Lori. (2019 September 30). "Binaural Beats Therapy: Benefits and How They Work. *Medical News Today*. www.medicalnewstoday.com/articles/320019.

Susana. (2019 May 27). Vibrational Frequency of Emotions - Where Do You Sit on the Scale? *Cosmic Minds*. www.cosmicminds.net/vibrational-frequency-of-emotions-where-do-you-sit-on-the-scale/.

The Chalkboard Staff. (2016 April 27). What Are the 7 Chakras + How They Function from Root to Crown. *The Chalkboard*. thechalkboardmag.com/understanding-the-chakras.

Tracey, Brian. (2010) *Goals!: How to Get Everything You Want- Faster than You Ever Thought Possible*. Brett Koehler Publishers.

University of West Alabama Online. (2019 June 27). The Science of Emotion: Exploring the Basics of Emotional Psychology. *UWA Online*. online.uwa.edu/news/emotional-psychology/.

University of West Alabama Online. (2019 May 17). Our Basic Emotions Infographic | List of Human Emotions. *UWA Online.* online.uwa.edu/infographics/basic-emotions/.

Weir, Kirsten. (2012). A Complex Emotion. *American Psychological Association,*(10), 64.

Wellmes, Deb. (2016 March 17). 7 Health Benefits of Vibroacoustic (Sound & Vibration) Therapy. *Wake up World.* wakeup-world.com/2016/03/18/7-health-benefits-of-vibroacoustic-sound-vibration-therapy/.

Wingo, Mary. (2016). *The Impact of the Human Stress Response: The Biological Origins of Human Stress (a Practical Stress Management Book about the Mind-Body Connection of Stress).* Roxwell Waterhouse.

Woodford, Chris. (2019 February 20). Sound - the Science of Waves, How They Travel, How We Use Them. *Explain That Stuff.* www.explainthatstuff.com/sound.html.

Yes Therapy Helps Staff. (2021 July 29). The Model of the 3 Brains: Reptilian, Limbic and Neocortex. *Yes, Therapy Helps!* en.yestherapyhelps.com/the-model-of-the-3-brains-reptilian-limbic-and-neocortex-11585.

Yoga for Beginners Staff. (n.d). Rhythmic Breathing Is Ideal for Breathing Practice for Beginners. *Yoga for Beginners- A Practical Guide.* www.yoga-for-beginners-a-practical-guide.com/rhythmic-breathing.html#:~:text=Benefits%201%20Breath%20is%20life%2C%20orhythmic%20breathing%20harmonises.

Yrizarry, Shannon. (2018 February 22). Why You Need to Clear Your Energy Field with Breathwork. *Daily Life.* dailylife.com/article/why-you-need-to-clear-your-energy-field-with-breath-work.

Zupan, B, et al. (2014). Affect recognition in traumatic brain injury responses to unimodal and multimodal media. *Journal of Head Trauma Rehabilitation,*(4), E1-E12.